Student Workbook

PACEMAKER®

Basic English
Composition

PEARSON
AGS Globe

Shoreview, MN

Pearson AGS Globe™ and Pacemaker® are trademarks, in the U.S. and/or in other countries, of Pearson Education, Inc. or its affiliate(s).

ISBN-13: 978-0-7854-6333-7
ISBN-10: 0-7854-6333-X

3 4 5 6 7 8 9 10 V036 11 10

1-800-992-0244
www.agsglobe.com

Table of Contents

Chapter 1   Writing Sentences

Workbook Activity 1   How a Sentence Begins and Ends
Workbook Activity 2   What Is the Purpose of a Sentence?
Workbook Activity 3   Look for the Subject and Predicate
Workbook Activity 4   Sentence Fragments
Workbook Activity 5   Run-On Sentences

Chapter 2   Writing Correct Sentences

Workbook Activity 6   Subject and Verb Agreement
Workbook Activity 7   Irregular Verbs and Verb Tenses
Workbook Activity 8   Verbs and Verb Phrases
Workbook Activity 9   Conjunctions Help Combine Ideas
Workbook Activity 10   Other Kinds of Conjunctions

Chapter 3   Writing Better Sentences

Workbook Activity 11   Using the Right Pronoun
Workbook Activity 12   Plurals and Possessives
Workbook Activity 13   Using Adjectives and Adverbs for Better Sentences
Workbook Activity 14   Using Adjectives and Adverbs to Compare
Workbook Activity 15   Identifying Prepositional Phrases

Chapter 4   Writing Paragraphs

Workbook Activity 16   Understanding Writing Prompts and Paragraph Prompts
Workbook Activity 17   Identifying Good Topic Sentences
Workbook Activity 18   Staying on the Topic
Workbook Activity 19   Choosing Strong Summaries and Conclusions

Chapter 5   Writing Better Paragraphs

Workbook Activity 20   Writing Strong Topic Sentences
Workbook Activity 21   Creating Interesting Sentences
Workbook Activity 22   Adding Transitional Words and Phrases
Workbook Activity 23   Improving Paragraph Drafts
Workbook Activity 24   Correcting Mistakes in Writing

Table of Contents, continued

Chapter 6   Writing to Explain

Workbook Activity 25   Writing a How-To Paragraph

Workbook Activity 26   Explaining What Something Means

Workbook Activity 27   Understanding How Two Things Are Alike and Different

Workbook Activity 28   Understanding When One Event Causes Another

Workbook Activity 29   Identifying Problems and Solutions

Chapter 7   Writing to Persuade

Workbook Activity 30   Learning About Opinions

Workbook Activity 31   Is That a Fact?

Workbook Activity 32   Persuading with Facts and Opinions

Workbook Activity 33   Ads That Convince

Chapter 8   Writing to Describe

Workbook Activity 34   Writing with Sense Appeal

Workbook Activity 35   Being Exact in Descriptions

Workbook Activity 36   Describing by Comparing

Workbook Activity 37   Writing Choices for Style

Chapter 9   Writing to Tell a Story

Workbook Activity 38   Story Time

Workbook Activity 39   What Happened Next?

Workbook Activity 40   Who Is the Storyteller?

Workbook Activity 41   When Did It Happen?

Workbook Activity 42   Creating Dialogue

Workbook Activity 43   Knowing When to Use Quotation Marks

Chapter 10   Writing for School

Workbook Activity 44   Writing a Short Answer to a Test Question

Workbook Activity 45   Planning an Essay Answer

Workbook Activity 46   Writing a Report

Chapter 11   Writing for Yourself

Workbook Activity 47   Create a Personal Letter

Workbook Activity 48   Take a Message

Workbook Activity 49   Understanding Electronic Mail (E-Mail) Messages

Table of Contents, continued

Chapter 12   Writing for the Workplace

Workbook Activity 50	Parts of a Business Letter
Workbook Activity 51	Addresses on Envelopes
Workbook Activity 52	Using Memo Form

Chapter 13   Preparing to Write a Report

Workbook Activity 53	Expressing Opinion in a Report
Workbook Activity 54	Topic Selection
Workbook Activity 55	Using Reference Materials
Workbook Activity 56	Searching the Internet
Workbook Activity 57	Notes
Workbook Activity 58	Correcting an Outline

Chapter 14   Writing the Final Report

Workbook Activity 59	Organizing Topics to Write a Report
Workbook Activity 60	Adding Transitions
Workbook Activity 61	Subject-Verb Agreement
Workbook Activity 62	Creating a Bibliography
Workbook Activity 63	Preparing to Publish

How a Sentence Begins and Ends

Directions Read each group of words. Find the sentences and write them on a separate sheet of paper. Capitalize the first word in each sentence. Put a punctuation mark at the end.

EXAMPLE   everyone in my family likes yogurt our favorite flavor is strawberry we often have yogurt for a snack

Everyone in my family likes yogurt.

Our favorite flavor is strawberry.

We often have yogurt for a snack.

1. in the spring we planted a garden we planted green peppers and squash first later we planted tomatoes

2. my grandmother sent me a CD for my birthday I wrote a letter to thank her she was pleased

3. my friends and I started a singing group we practice five times a month I think we need more practice

4. today it rained the streets were flooded we could not get our car out of the garage

5. there was an announcement in the newspaper about an upcoming concert tickets go on sale next week I would love to go to that concert

6. yesterday my sister went to the bank she wanted to deposit her paycheck she also wanted to get some quarters for the machines at the laundry

7. I saw an announcement on the bulletin board the coach is having tryouts for the soccer team should my friend and I go

8. every year the garden club has a sale the club members offer many different kinds of plants they tell customers all about the plants

9. what two things must a writer do first a writer must think of an idea to write about he or she also must decide how to write about the idea

10. my new digital camera takes amazing pictures I love photography I would like to take a class to learn more about it

What Is the Purpose of a Sentence?

Directions Add correct punctuation at the end of each sentence. Write the purpose of each sentence on the line. Choose from the following:

Statement   **Question**   **Command**   **Exclamation**

EXAMPLE The ship leaves at noon. _____statement_____

1. Having a bank account is important _____

2. What kind of bank account do you have _____

3. Can you have more than one type of account _____

4. Yes, you can _____

5. I have enough money to buy a CD player _____

6. Eliza explained that she just opened her account _____

7. I am saving to buy a car when I graduate _____

8. Please tell me when I have enough _____

9. How much is enough _____

10. You should know soon _____

11. I have plenty of time to decide _____

12. Mrs. Choy has two accounts _____

13. Does she have a checking account _____

14. Please explain how to open a checking account _____

15. What is the purpose of a checking account _____

16. Can you use a checking account in place of cash _____

17. It is safer than cash _____

18. Derek, write me a check _____

19. How do you choose the correct bank _____

20. Do research before choosing a bank _____

Look for the Subject and Predicate

Directions Underline the subject of each sentence with one line. If the subject is understood, write *you* and underline it. Underline the predicate with two lines.

EXAMPLE The new year gives many people new hope.

1. Dad plans to lose weight.

2. Many people diet in January.

3. Drink at least eight glasses of water a day.

4. Fruits and vegetables give us many vitamins and minerals.

5. Fats and oils should be eaten moderately.

6. Whole grains provide fiber.

7. Most dieters do not stick to a strict diet.

8. They get too hungry.

9. Eat plenty of good, nutritious food.

10. An exercise program also takes off pounds.

Directions Underline the verb or verb phrase in each sentence. Decide the tense of the verb. Write the correct letter on the line.

A present **B** past **C** future

EXAMPLE Last year I made a resolution on New Year's Eve. ____B____

11. For a week, I kept my room clean. _____

12. My dog Lucky messed up the bed. _____

13. My little brother tracked in mud. _____

14. Today it looks neat and clean. _____

15. That usually lasts about ten minutes. _____

16. Next year, I will make a different resolution. _____

17. I will exercise every day. _____

18. Jose runs for exercise. _____

19. Last year he ran a marathon. _____

20. I will never run twenty-six miles! _____

Sentence Fragments

Directions Label each group of words as a *sentence* or a *fragment*. If the fragment needs a subject, write *subject*. If it needs a predicate, write *predicate*.

EXAMPLE Landed on the ground. _____ fragment, subject _____

1. The cute little dog. _____

2. Leaped into the air. _____

3. Chased the Frisbee like a pro. _____

4. The dog's owner. _____

5. Threw the plastic disc gracefully. _____

6. A family on a picnic looked up in surprise. _____

7. The three children. _____

8. Laughed at the leaping dog. _____

9. They cheered when he caught it in his mouth. _____

10. A bunch of ducks on the pond. _____

Directions Correct each fragment. Add words to make it a complete sentence. Write your sentences on the lines.

EXAMPLE The swimming pool at the park.

The swimming pool at the park has a water slide. _____

11. The highest diving board. _____

_____

12. A very small boy. _____

_____

13. Looked up at the boy with concern. _____

_____

14. Watched to see what would happen. _____

_____

15. Jumped into the water. _____

_____

Run-On Sentences

Directions Read each group of words. Three sentences have been run together. Find the beginning and the end of each complete thought. Write the three sentences on the lines. Capitalize and punctuate each sentence.

EXAMPLE Derek loves baseball he plays every Saturday he goes to a lot of games.

    Derek loves baseball.

    He plays every Saturday.

    He goes to a lot of games.

The baseball game begins at 7:30 p.m. pick me up at 6:30 I don't want to be late.

1. _____

2. _____

3. _____

The Wolves are playing the Cougars the Wolves have won six games the Cougars have won four.

4. _____

5. _____

6. _____

The batter hit the ball hard the left fielder ran back the ball went over the fence.

7. _____

8. _____

9. _____

It was a home run the crowd cheered wildly people love to see home runs.

10. _____

11. _____

12. _____

The batter jogged around the bases he waved to the crowd his teammates met him at home plate.

13. _____

14. _____

15. _____

Subject and Verb Agreement

Directions Read each sentence. The subject is in bold. If the subject is singular, circle *singular*. If it is plural, circle *plural*. Then underline the correct form of the verb to finish the sentence.

EXAMPLE Most **children** (<u>like</u>, likes) clowns.   singular   (plural)

1. **Eliza** (throws, throw) a party every year.   singular   plural

2. **Both** of my friends (is, are) going to the party.   singular   plural

3. **She** (makes, make) the best snacks you ever tasted.   singular   plural

4. Her **house** (has, have) a recreation room.   singular   plural

5. **Jason** and **Eliza** (loves, love) parties.   singular   plural

6. **They** (dances, dance) well together.   singular   plural

7. **Brandon** always (gets, get) there early.   singular   plural

8. **Everyone** (knows, know) to come on time.   singular   plural

9. Eliza's **father** (comes, come) downstairs at 12.   singular   plural

10. **All** of Eliza's friends (goes, go) home then.   singular   plural

Directions Read each sentence. On each line, write the form of the verb in parentheses that agrees with the subject.

EXAMPLE He and I _____hope_____ to receive many gifts. (hopes, hope)

11. Both Amber and Eliza _____ parties. (enjoys, enjoy)

12. Everybody _____ about the graduation party. (knows, know)

13. Each of the girls _____ very good cakes. (bakes, bake)

14. One of the soccer players _____ football, too. (likes, like)

15. The dog _____ over the gate all the time. (jumps, jump)

16. Several girls _____ Eliza every night. (calls, call)

17. Many people _____ to watch the parade. (stays, stay)

18. A few of them _____ along with the music. (claps, clap)

19. Either Derek or Brandon _____ to drive. (plans, plan)

20. Neither Amber nor Eliza _____ a ride. (wants, want)

Irregular Verbs and Verb Tenses

Directions Read each sentence. Underline the verb. Identify its tense.
Write *present, past, future, present perfect, past perfect,* or *future perfect* on
the line.

EXAMPLE Jody has taught swimming lessons. _____present perfect_____

1. Ramon took a picture of the sunset. _____

2. His photo won a contest. _____

3. The winner did a dance. _____

4. We have eaten out a lot lately. _____

5. The twins go to Mel's Diner every Monday. _____

6. I had seen them earlier at the mall. _____

7. Will you drive me home? _____

8. My favorite show will have begun. _____

9. Have you seen the keys? _____

10. This accident has taught me a lesson. _____

11. I have plenty of time to decide. _____

Directions Complete each sentence by writing a perfect tense of the verb
in parentheses on the line. Remember to add *has, have, had,* or *will have* to
the past participle.

EXAMPLE Everyone but me ____has gone____ to the art show already. (go)

12. The bus left as soon as the last student _____ a seat.
(take)

13. By tomorrow, I _____ my dog that trick. (teach)

14. For the last year, she _____ to the nursing home
every Saturday. (go)

15. Carl and Ted _____ each other since kindergarten.
(know)

Verbs and Verb Phrases

Directions Write the verb or verb phrase in each sentence on the line.
Then underline each helping verb.

EXAMPLE I should have helped you with dinner.   <u>should have</u> helped _____

1. She will arrive late because of traffic. _____
2. Derek has visited us every spring. _____
3. Eliza is watching videos with Derek. _____
4. They stopped at the store. _____
5. Amber had bought a dress for the party. _____
6. Derek should have noticed right away. _____
7. My job will start next week. _____
8. The editor has asked for nature photos. _____
9. That ad ran for two weeks straight. _____
10. Photography can be an interesting hobby. _____

Directions Read each sentence. If it uses tenses correctly, write *correct* on
the line. If it does not use tenses correctly, rewrite the sentence to fix it.

EXAMPLE: When you explained it, it seems easy.
   <u>When you explain it, it seems easy.</u>
   OR   <u>When you explained it, it seemed easy.</u>

11. I tiptoe up the front steps, but the squeaky door gave me away.

_____

12. My parents always worry when I was late.

_____

13. When I have my own cell phone, I will call them at 11.

_____

14. That way they knew that I am all right.

_____

15. The dog never gets mad at me, but my parents often do.

_____

Conjunctions Help Combine Ideas

Directions Combine each group of sentences into one longer sentence.
Use conjunctions and punctuation correctly. Make sure the subjects and
verbs agree.

EXAMPLE Monday it snowed. Tuesday it snowed. Wednesday it snowed.
Monday, Tuesday, and Wednesday it snowed.

1. Derek was bored. Derek was tired. Derek was hungry.

   _____

2. He shoved his books into his locker. He slammed the door. He ran to
   the exit.

   _____

3. Amber likes shopping. She also likes dancing. She likes cooking, too.

   _____

4. June has a deep laugh. Grace has a high, shrill laugh.

   _____

5. Hou sings very well. He could win the talent contest.

   _____

Directions Underline the conjunction or conjunctions in each sentence.
Add any commas that are needed.

EXAMPLE Nan sent postcards <u>but</u> she got home before they arrived.

6. Will you have toast or pancakes with your eggs?

7. I love breakfast but I usually rush through it.

8. I always have people to see places to go and things to do.

9. We should relax and look around us but we never have time.

10. We should either do less or sleep more.

11. Not only kids but also their parents are stressed out.

12. Some of us are taking yoga and that relaxes us.

13. Grandpa and Grandma walk or dance for exercise.

14. He tried to teach me the foxtrot but I was too clumsy.

15. Take time to relax or you will not be happy.

Other Kinds of Conjunctions

Directions Underline the dependent clause in each sentence once. Underline the subordinating conjunction in each sentence twice.

EXAMPLE Help me carry this plant outside <u>before you go home</u>.

1. I go to the flower show whenever it comes to town.

2. While you are at camp, you will learn outdoor skills.

3. Because he loves the great outdoors, Brian enjoys camp.

4. When it snows, we can build a snowman.

5. Venus attended design school so that she could make her own clothes.

6. You will find it if you look harder.

7. Until we find the key, we aren't going anywhere.

8. Since he started dance class, Al has lost ten pounds.

9. I will set the table while you finish making dinner.

10. Although she loves lasagna, Mom doesn't make it herself.

Directions Combine each pair of sentences using one of the subordinating conjunctions in the Word Bank. Write each new sentence on the line. Use correct punctuation.

Word Bank
after
although
because
if
since
when
while

11. The storm was over. We went outside.

   _____

12. Dinner is ready. We can eat.

   _____

13. Cathy got new sneakers. Her old ones had worn out.

   _____

14. You do my chores for a week. I will tutor you in math.

   _____

15. I love dogs. I am allergic to them.

   _____

Using the Right Pronoun

Directions Change each noun in bold to a pronoun. Write the pronoun on the line. Remember, a pronoun must agree in number and gender with the word it replaces.

EXAMPLES Where did **Mary** go? _____ she
Nancy and Joan are sisters. _____ They

1. **Derek and Eliza** agreed to meet for lunch. _____

2. Derek saw Eliza after **Eliza's** English class. _____

3. Mr. Braun gave **Mr. Braun's** class a test. _____

4. Eliza had trouble with **the test.** _____

5. **Eliza** talked to Mr. Braun about her concern. _____

6. Derek paced because **Derek** hated to be late. _____

7. "I'm sorry to make you wait," Eliza said to **Derek.** _____

8. The special was pizza, and Derek loved **pizza.** _____

9. Amber saved a seat for **Derek and Eliza.** _____

10. She wondered why **her friends** were late. _____

Directions Circle the correct pronoun in parentheses. Write *subject* if the pronoun is a subject. Write *object* if it is an object.

EXAMPLE James has given (I, me) his old racket. _____ object

11. (She, Her) loves taco salad more than chocolate. _____

12. Offer the tea to Marius and (they, them). _____

13. Derek and (they, them) walked home. _____

14. (He, Him) looks nervous to me. _____

15. Brad said that you could go with (him and me, he and I). _____

Plurals and Possessives

Directions Decide whether each noun is singular or plural. Write *singular* or *plural* on the line beside each noun. Then write the possessive form of the noun.

EXAMPLE dogs _____ plural, dogs' _____

1. video _____
2. wife _____
3. people _____
4. men _____
5. toothbrush _____

6. suitcases _____
7. fox _____
8. coaches _____
9. feet _____
10. radios _____

Directions The apostrophes have been left out of these possessive phrases. Read each phrase and write it on the line. Put an apostrophe in the correct place.

EXAMPLES the ladys purse _____ the lady's purse _____
the mens club _____ the men's club _____

11. the wolfs howl _____
12. the calves pen _____
13. Ambers dog Lucky _____
14. the childrens room _____
15. the Smiths vacation _____

16. a books cover _____
17. the cities parks _____
18. the peoples choice _____
19. the familys car _____
20. two cats food _____

Using Adjectives and Adverbs for Better Sentences

Directions Read the sentences. Write an adjective or an adverb on each line to complete each sentence.

EXAMPLE The __small__ boy sat __quietly__ in the corner.

1. I like _____ ice cream with _____ sauce on it.

2. Derek drives _____ in _____ weather.

3. The _____ girl asked Derek to go to the _____ movie.

4. The _____ sprinter was _____ after a _____ run.

5. The _____ exam lasted _____ hours and was _____ difficult.

6. The _____ library has _____ books that are _____ for research.

7. Our _____ dinner at Al's Beef is the _____ fish.

8. The flowers were _____ and _____.

9. On a _____ day, we _____ go to the _____ beach.

10. The evening ended _____ after he _____ spilled his drink.

11. A _____ cat meowed _____ from the treetop.

12. A _____ cab sped by and splashed me _____ with dirty water.

13. _____ gifts are _____ welcome.

14. Isaac was _____ surprised by the _____ announcement.

15. A _____ horse is _____ relaxed on the trail.

Using Adjectives and Adverbs to Compare

Directions Choose the correct form of the word in parentheses. Write your answer on the line.

EXAMPLE Belle is _____younger_____ than Molly is. (younger, youngest)

1. Which of the two pizzas do you like _____? (better, best)

2. An apple is _____ than a cracker. (more filling, most filling)

3. Which is the _____ expensive of those three dresses? (less, least)

4. The movie was _____ than the book. (worse, worst)

5. Derek is the _____ person in the group. (taller, tallest)

6. My mom drives _____ than my dad. (slower, slowest)

Directions Write a sentence using each adjective or adverb correctly. Use the form listed beside the adjective or adverb.

EXAMPLE terrible—comparative
The second song was even more terrible than the first one.

7. wise—superlative

_____

8. good/well—comparative

_____

9. much—superlative

_____

10. quickly—comparative

_____

Identifying Prepositional Phrases

Directions Circle the prepositional phrase in each sentence. Write
adjective on the line if the phrase is used as an adjective. Write *adverb* if it
is used as an adverb.

EXAMPLE The soldiers received packages (from home.) _____ adjective _____

1. She found the cat under the table. _____

2. Eliza asked if she could go with us. _____

3. A box of oranges came in the mail. _____

4. He ate cereal with fresh fruit. _____

5. Our visitors will arrive at 10 A.M. _____

6. I go to the library most Saturdays. _____

7. A letter from my dad came today. _____

8. The lost glove was lying behind the radiator. _____

9. Our history club attended a lecture on
   the Civil War. _____

10. The land between the cities has become crowded. _____

11. Jules led a demonstration against the war. _____

12. Several small plates broke during the move. _____

13. The treats for the party are pizza and cake. _____

14. A yellow cake with chocolate icing is best. _____

15. We will feed around 30 people. _____

Understanding Writing Prompts and Paragraph Prompts

Directions Read each writing prompt. Fill in the missing information in the chart.

Writing Prompt	Purpose of Your Answer	Audience	Topic	Key Words
1. Write an essay to compare life in 1800 to life today.				

Writing Prompt	Purpose of Your Answer	Audience	Topic	Key Words
2. Write a paragraph to describe the stories of Edgar Allan Poe.				

Directions The sentences below can be used to write a paragraph. Read the sentences. Decide how they should be ordered. Number the sentences in order.

_____ **3.** He first became popular as the star of comedies such as *Big*.

_____ **4.** His many awards prove that Hanks is among our most gifted actors.

_____ **5.** Later, he went on to star in many major dramas.

_____ **6.** Tom Hanks is one of Hollywood's finest, best-liked actors.

_____ **7.** He became the first actor since 1938 to win the Academy Award for Best Actor two years in a row.

Identifying Good Topic Sentences

Directions Read each pair of topic sentences. Put a check mark (✓) on the line next to the better topic sentence in each pair.

1. _____ **A** Raising cattle is a risky business.
   _____ **B** Cattle are a source of food.

2. _____ **A** There are many kinds of office furniture.
   _____ **B** Select your office desk and chair carefully.

3. _____ **A** An encyclopedia can be used a lot of ways.
   _____ **B** An encyclopedia is a valuable reference book.

4. _____ **A** Swimming is my favorite summer sport.
   _____ **B** Swimming is for fun and for sport.

5. _____ **A** There are lots of good careers.
   _____ **B** Choosing a career is an important decision.

6. _____ **A** I enjoy many different TV programs.
   _____ **B** "Medical Makeover" is my favorite reality show.

7. _____ **A** The zoo is home to a wide variety of animals.
   _____ **B** Monkeys live happily in a zoo.

8. _____ **A** Being on a team offers several surprising benefits.
   _____ **B** Throughout history, people have played team sports.

9. _____ **A** A rattle snake is a dangerous snake.
   _____ **B** There are a number of poisonous snakes.

10. _____ **A** Malls draw shoppers with their variety and convenience.
    _____ **B** Malls are good places to shop.

Staying on the Topic

Directions Read the topic sentences for Paragraphs 1 and 2. Write the letters of the details that belong under each topic sentence.

> **A** They saw elephants and seals.
>
> **B** It travels by land.
>
> **C** It avoids traffic jams on highways.
>
> **D** They saw a polar bear swimming.
>
> **E** David watched the giraffes eat, and Fran saw the baby donkey get a bath.
>
> **F** A train can take you places much faster than a car.

Paragraph 1	**Paragraph 2**
David and Fran went to the zoo.	A train is a form of transportation.
1. _____	4. _____
2. _____	5. _____
3. _____	6. _____

Directions In each paragraph, one sentence does not relate to the paragraph topic. Find this sentence and cross it out.

7. It was a beautiful day. Juan decided to take his sailboat out on the lake. He sailed for an hour. Juan had homework to do. He passed several other sailboats while on the lake.

8. Space exploration is very important to the United Sates. It allows the country to explore other planets. Space exploration also enables this country to set up space satellites. Mexico is not involved in space exploration. The United States has launched many space missions.

9. Exercise is important for a healthy body. Reading is an enjoyable hobby. Jogging and swimming are excellent forms of exercise. Some people like to work out at a gym. Walking is an exercise for all ages.

10. Cake decorating takes time and patience. The icing must be smooth. Then, you must add a small amount of coloring to a small amount of icing. You must do this for each different color you use. Everyone will enjoy the cake. Using your colored icing, you decorate the cake with a picture or words

Choosing Strong Summaries and Conclusions

Directions Read each paragraph. Choose the better summary or conclusion for it. Put a check mark next to this sentence.

1. It is important to choose safe toys for children. Toys that are sharp or too small are not appropriate for babies or small children. Toys for older children should provide many hours of entertainment.

   _____ **A** Books for children are also needed.
   _____ **B** Well-chosen toys will only benefit your children.

2. Beginning swimmers are required to develop a variety of skills. Each skill encourages the swimmer to be comfortable in the water by building a swimmer's confidence.

   _____ **A** Beginning swimmers are not expected to know every swimming stroke.
   _____ **B** A swimmer's confidence will enable him or her to learn any swimming stroke.

3. There are many kinds of TV game shows. Though the shows are different, they all give away money, prizes, or both. The people who try to win are called contestants.

   _____ **A** To win money, contestants answer questions or do certain tasks.
   _____ **B** It is fun to win.

4. A boa constrictor is a large, dangerous snake. Boas can grow to be 20 feet long. Some weigh as much as 140 pounds. A boa typically crushes its prey and then swallows it in one gulp.

   _____ **A** You cannot be too careful around a boa constrictor!
   _____ **B** Another dangerous snake is the water moccasin.

5. Our museums are windows to the past. Many science museums exhibit the bones of dinosaurs that lived millions of years ago. In art museums, paintings show what life was like in past centuries. Historical museums show clothing and other objects from long ago.

   _____ **A** We have an excellent science museum in our city.
   _____ **B** We can learn so much about the past in museums.

Writing Strong Topic Sentences

Directions Improve these topic sentences. Change words around. Add more details.

1. You have to do things like practice if you want to be good at baseball.

_____

_____

2. Novels that tell why people do things are good.

_____

_____

3. Old things that you can find in attics are interesting.

_____

_____

4. Different spices go into a lot of gourmet foods.

_____

_____

5. If one wants a good job, then one should have the skills to do it.

_____

_____

6. Swimmers ought to know rules that will help them to be safe.

_____

_____

7. If you want to enjoy something, look at a sunset.

_____

_____

8. Insects do things that human beings often do.

_____

_____

Creating Interesting Sentences

Directions Rewrite each sentence by changing the word order. Find a different word or phrase in the sentence to put at the beginning. Capitalize the first word and use end punctuation.

EXAMPLE In the fall, the family usually goes camping.
Usually, the family goes camping in the fall.

1. We seldom watch TV in the summer.

_____

2. We are usually too busy with outdoor activities.

_____

3. The weather is always sunny and warm in this area.

_____

4. We have not had much rain in our town lately.

_____

5. I heard thunder suddenly rumbling in the background.

_____

6. Everyone immediately was sure that we would have rain.

_____

7. We opened the door and looked outside slowly.

_____

8. The thunder stopped after a few minutes.

_____

9. The sky was clear as far as we could see at that moment.

_____

10. We will get some rain someday soon.

_____

Adding Transitional Words and Phrases

Directions Rewrite these paragraphs to make them more interesting. Add transitional words or phrases such as *then, first, meanwhile, later, next, before, finally, also, at last,* or *in the meantime.*

1. Derek walked onto the tennis court. He was ready to serve. He tossed the ball into the air. He hit it hard. He really wanted to win the match.

_____

_____

_____

2. Amber watched the waves coming in. She looked for her parents. She saw them. She decided to hold their hands. The ocean was rough today.

_____

_____

_____

3. Computers do many things to help us. They keep banking records. They solve difficult math problems. They even control traffic lights.

_____

_____

_____

4. Brandon studied the pitcher carefully. It was his turn to bat. A hit would bring in the winning run. He stepped up to the plate. His eyes followed the ball until it met his bat. He knew he had helped win the game.

_____

_____

_____

5. Eliza wanted to make cookies for the bake sale. She turned on the oven. She got the ingredients she would need. She found a large bowl and a spoon. Eliza mixed the ingredients. She spooned the cookie dough onto the cookie sheet and put it in the oven to bake.

_____

_____

Improving Paragraph Drafts

Directions Read each paragraph. Cross out a sentence that does not belong. Add two new sentences to give each paragraph enough support. Write the new sentences on the lines.

1. I try hard to keep my room organized. All my clothes are neatly folded and put away. My little brother, on the other hand, is a slob.

2. _____

3. _____

4. My friend Carrie really cares about others. She enjoys singing. Carrie works every Saturday at a homeless shelter.

5. _____

6. _____

7. With just a little effort, you can make friends. It is not pleasant to have enemies. When you meet someone, smile and give the person a compliment.

8. _____

9. _____

10. There is much to see in the night sky. The moon changes through the month, growing full and then narrow. You should not look at the sun directly.

11. _____

12. _____

13. A dictionary is loaded with all sorts of useful information. It gives the meanings of words as well as their spellings and pronunciations. A thesaurus lists synonyms and antonyms for many words.

14. _____

15. _____

Correcting Mistakes in Writing

Directions Read the paragraph. Each sentence contains one or more mistakes. Rewrite the sentences correctly on the lines below.

1. Some citizens treet our city to carelessly. **2.** Many people, for example, still drops liter in the streets. **3.** others pollutes the air by burning trash. **4.** some citizens even leave broke appliances in vacant lots. **5.** others let they dogs roam and do not clean up after him. **6.** A few irresponsible people damaging bildings. **7.** for example, they draw and write on their. **8.** They may even breaking windows. **9.** A clean city give we something to be proud of. **10.** How beautiful our city wold be if people only took care of it!

1. _____

2. _____

3. _____

4. _____

5. _____

6. _____

7. _____

8. _____

9. _____

10. _____

Writing a How-To Paragraph

Directions Read the following how-to paragraph. Then write sentences to answer the questions.

Shopping for an Automobile

Buying your first automobile is a big decision that calls for careful planning. Your first step is deciding how much money you can spend. Count your cash and visit a bank to find out how much you can borrow. Now, with a price in mind, examine the automobiles in that price range. Make a list of your most important criteria. You may want a car with airbags. You may need a car with four doors. A car that has a warranty might be most important to you. When you have a favorite, you will want to take that car for a test drive. Most people ask an auto mechanic to check a car they are thinking about buying. All of these steps lead up to the day you make a decision and drive your car home.

1. What is the paragraph telling you how to do?

_____

_____

2. What is the first step in shopping for an automobile?

_____

_____

3. Underline three transitional words or phrases in the paragraph.

4. Write three things that the writer tells you to do before you purchase an automobile.

_____

_____

_____

5. Is the last sentence of the paragraph a summary or a conclusion? Explain your answer.

_____

_____

Explaining What Something Means

Directions Read the paragraph. Then answer the questions below it.

A convertible is a car with a top that can be removed or lowered. In every other way, a convertible is a typical car. It has four wheels, a windshield, seats, and so on. Yet, unlike a regular car, it makes the driver feel adventurous. There is something glamorous and thrilling about the idea of speeding along with the wind in your hair. When you think about a convertible, what do you picture? You probably think of a sporty, red little car that zips along. You picture yourself in sunglasses, enjoying a beautiful spring or summer day. A car may just be transportation, but a convertible sounds like a good time.

1. What does this paragraph define?

_____

2. What is the dictionary definition for this thing?

_____

_____

3. What are three details the writer added that explain what sets this thing apart from all others of its kind?

_____

_____

_____

4. How does your imagination help you understand the meaning of the thing?

_____

_____

_____

5. Does the paragraph end with a summary or a conclusion?

_____

Understanding How Two Things Are Alike and Different

Directions Read each sentence below. Think about how the words in italic type are related. Find a word in the Word Bank that is related to the underlined word in the same way. The first sentence has been done for you.

EXAMPLE *Hat* is to *head* as <u>glove</u> is to <u>hand</u>.

	Word Bank
	automobile
	cow
	hand
	neck
	riverbed
	writer

1. *Colt* is to *horse* as <u>calf</u> is to _____.

2. *Saw* is to *carpenter* as <u>pen</u> is to _____.

3. *Pilot* is to *airplane* as <u>driver</u> is to _____.

4. *Blood* is to *veins* as <u>water</u> is to _____.

5. *Hand* is to *wrist* as <u>head</u> is to _____.

Directions Write a sentence about each item above. In your sentence, use the four related words. Compare how two things are alike.

EXAMPLE To stay warm, it is just as important to wear a hat on your head as it is to wear gloves on your hands.

6. _____
   _____

7. _____
   _____

8. _____
   _____

9. _____
   _____

10. _____
    _____

Understanding When One Event Causes Another

Directions Read each set of sentences. Write *reasonable* if the relationship between the two events is reasonable. Write *not reasonable* if one event does not cause the other.

1. Spring temperatures warm the soil.
As a result, seeds begin to sprout.

_____

2. Farmers fertilize their crops.
Therefore, they spray insecticides.

_____

3. No rain falls for weeks.
Thus, the crops do not grow.

_____

4. Farmers pump water from a river.
Consequently, they use it to water their crops.

_____

5. Days grow short in autumn.
As a result, farmers harvest crops even after dark falls.

_____

Directions After each event, write two possible causes.

EXAMPLE The corn crop this year was the biggest ever.
The summer was warm and wet.   Insect pests and diseases were controlled.

6. People put less garbage into landfills this year.

_____

_____

7. Fewer people died in car accidents this year.

_____

_____

8. Fewer Americans took a vacation this year.

_____

_____

_____

9. Most American homes have at least one computer in them.

_____

_____

10. A stoplight was installed at the entrance to the mall.

_____

_____

Identifying Problems and Solutions

Directions Read the paragraph. Then answer the questions below.

This year, I want to be a starter for our basketball team. Last year, I spent most of every game warming the bench. To get playing time, I need to improve my skills and show the coach I am better. Practicing my free throws and dribbling in the driveway every afternoon will help. I can also play pickup games with my friends in the park. We have agreed that we will play every weekend. Finally, I have signed up for the park district basketball league. My park team will have a coach and play ten games. That experience should help me improve a lot. Next November, I'm sure to impress the coach!

1. What problem does the writer have? State the problem in your own words.

_____

_____

2. What is the solution to this problem?

_____

_____

3. List three things the writer plans to do to put this solution into effect.

_____

_____

_____

4. Does the paragraph end with a conclusion or a summary? Explain.

_____

5. Write a different final sentence for this paragraph.

_____

_____

Learning About Opinions

Directions Each of the following paragraphs gives an opinion. Read each paragraph. Then answer the questions about it.

Fast food is making Americans overweight and unhealthy. Most fast food is full of unhealthy fat or sugar—two foods we should not eat often. Over the last 20 years, Americans have begun eating out more and more. Today, we eat more food in restaurants than at home. Fast food is our favorite junk food habit. This eating habit has caused many Americans to become dangerously overweight. Being overweight has been linked to illnesses such as diabetes and heart trouble.

1. What is the writer's opinion of fast food?

_____

2–4. What are three reasons the writer gives for thinking this? _____

_____

_____

_____

5. Do you agree or disagree with the writer? Tell why.

_____

It is a mistake to cut down the tropical rain forests. When the trees are gone, no roots hold the soil in place. The soil washes away, causing the land to be like a desert. Many animals live in the rain forest. They lose their homes when the forest is cut down. The balance of nature changes in a bad way. Most important, tropical forests produce a lot of oxygen. Without them, our atmosphere will not be healthy.

6. What is the writer's opinion about rain forests?

_____

7–9. What are three reasons the writer gives for thinking this? _____

_____

_____

_____

10. Do you agree or disagree with the writer? Tell why.

_____

Is That a Fact?

Directions Read the statements. Write *fact* beside each fact. Write *opinion* beside each opinion.

EXAMPLES Cats make the best pets.　　　　　　opinion
　　　　　　I have owned three cats in all.　　　　fact

1. Summer is the best season.

_____

2. Pine trees are evergreens.

_____

3. Almonds are the perfect food.

_____

4. No one likes a crybaby.

_____

5. Hector scored 12 goals this season.

_____

6. Hector is the best player on the team.

_____

7. Soccer is more fun than football.

_____

8. Snakes are reptiles.

_____

9. You must be crazy if you keep a pet snake.

_____

10. The yard has fewer weeds this year.

_____

Directions These opinions are too general. Rewrite each opinion on the line. Use a qualifying word or phrase from the Word Bank.

Word Bank	
in my opinion	*probably*
may	*seems to*
many	*sometimes*

11. It will be cold on the field.

_____

12. Parents do not understand their teens.

_____

13. Plasma TVs are the best TVs.

_____

14. Music soothes the soul.

_____

15. Lack of sleep makes people grouchy.

_____

Persuading with Facts and Opinions

Directions Choose one of the topics below. Write your opinion about the topic beside 1. Then list three reasons for your opinion beside 2–4. Finally write a conclusion or summary sentence beside 5.

curfew   ads in school   banning transfats

Topic Sentence

1. _____

_____

Supporting Details

2. _____

_____

3. _____

_____

4. _____

_____

Summary or Conclusion Sentence

5. _____

_____

Directions Use your sentences from above to write a persuasive paragraph on the lines below.

_____

_____

_____

_____

_____

_____

_____

_____

Ads That Convince

Directions Choose one of the topics below. Think of an ad that will convince students to take action. Answer the questions below.

Keep the school grounds clean.   Be on time for class.   Treat others with respect.

1. What will be the purpose of your ad?

   _____

2. What reasons will you give to convince students you are right?

   _____

   _____

   _____

   _____

3. What pictures could you use to get your idea across?

   _____

   _____

4. What slogan can you use to get attention and make your point?

   _____

5. What do you want students to remember about your ad?

   _____

Directions Write your ad in the space below. Sketch in pictures where they should go. Put your slogan where it is easy to see.

Writing with Sense Appeal

Directions Complete each sentence. Add words that appeal to the sense listed in parentheses.

EXAMPLE <u>The smell of cut grass</u> filled the air after the yard was mowed.   (smell)

1. In the distance, we could hear _____.
   (hearing)

2. The snake's scales felt _____.
   (touch)

3. The milk shake tasted _____.
   (taste)

4. The lizard _____.
   (sight)

5. A loaf of baking bread smelled _____.
   (smell)

Directions Alliteration appeals to the sense of hearing. Write a sentence or a phrase using each word below. Include several words that begin with the same sound.

EXAMPLE rose   <u>a ruby red rose in a rusty vase</u>

6. bees_____

7. swimming _____

8. limousine _____

9. magic _____

10. jelly_____

Being Exact in Descriptions

Directions Write specific nouns, verbs, or adjectives on the lines to complete each sentence. Make the description exact and vivid.

EXAMPLE A <u>graceful</u> dancer <u>glided</u> across the floor.

1. The radio _____ out the _____ news.

2. A _____ cowboy _____ into town.

3. In the hallway, students _____ between classes.

4. _____ soldiers returned to the _____.

5. We saw newborn _____ sleeping in a _____.

Directions Read each group of words. Write the words in order from most general to most specific.

EXAMPLE jeans   clothing   pants   _____clothing, pants, jeans_____

6. scientist   career   biologist   _____

7. bag   container   backpack   _____

8. buck   wildlife   deer   _____

9. singer   soprano   musician   _____

10. building   place   post office   _____

Describing by Comparing

Directions Read each figure of speech. Circle the letter of the word that correctly names the figure of speech.

1. The room was as quiet as a graveyard.
   A metaphor   **B** simile   **C** personification   **D** exaggeration

2. The kids were so excited they jumped to the moon.
   A metaphor   **B** simile   **C** personification   **D** exaggeration

3. Maggie is a peach to do this for us.
   A metaphor   **B** simile   **C** personification   **D** exaggeration

4. The old engine coughed and complained then sputtered to life.
   A metaphor   **B** simile   **C** personification   **D** exaggeration

5. You look like something the cat just dragged in.
   A metaphor   **B** simile   **C** personification   **D** exaggeration

Directions Add a figure of speech to complete each sentence. Write the kind of figure of speech listed in parentheses.

EXAMPLE On her birthday, Joan was <u>as happy as a cat with cream</u>. (simile)

6. That Ferris wheel is so big _____.
   (exaggeration)

7. To the king, the princess is _____.
   (metaphor)

8. The sun and moon _____
   for the sky. (personification)

9. Victor spends money like _____.
   (simile)

10. The music was so loud _____.
    (exaggeration)

Writing Choices for Style

Directions Read the topic sentence below. Add three detail sentences and
a conclusion to make a paragraph. Then answer the questions below.

Joe and Mandy thought that Miss Iris, who lived in the old house on the
hill, was a witch.

_____

_____

_____

_____

_____

1. Find three specific words you used. Write them on the line.

   _____

2. What are two words you could make more specific? Underline them.
   Then write replacement words on the line.

   _____

3. Count the words in each sentence. How many long sentences (more
   than 10 words) are there? How many short sentences?

   _____

4. Have you used figures of speech? If so, circle them. If you have not,
   add at least one to the paragraph.

   _____

5. What is your paragraph about? Have you described it well?
   If not, add more description on these lines.

   _____

   _____

   _____

Story Time

Directions Write a story about something that happened to you. First, fill in the story map to tell about the parts of your story.

What your story is about:_____

Characters (who it is about):_____

Setting (where and when it happened):_____

Plot (what happened):

1. _____

2. _____

3. _____

4. _____

5. _____

Directions Write your story on the lines below. Use the story map information. Be sure to write a good topic sentence and a conclusion or summary at the end.

_____

_____

_____

_____

_____

_____

_____

_____

_____

_____

_____

_____

What Happened Next?

Directions Read the story below. Underline transitions that show when events happened. Then list the story events in order on the lines.

Geronimo was a great Apache warrior and fighter. He was born in 1829 in the Southwest. In 1876, he and his people were forced to move from their homes to some poor land in east Arizona. Geronimo and some followers then fled into Mexico. Over the next ten years, he escaped from reservations many times. Armies never seemed to be able to track him down. When Geronimo finally surrendered in 1886, he had become the last Indian still fighting against the U.S. government. He died in Oklahoma in 1909, a prisoner far from home.

1. _____

2. _____

3. _____

4. _____

5. _____

Who Is the Storyteller?

Directions The story below is written in third-person point of view. Read the story. Then rewrite it on the lines below using first-person point of view.

Callie was very hungry. She went to her locker to get her lunch, but it was not there. She wondered what had happened to it. Callie thought about her morning. Then she remembered that she had left her lunch on the counter at home. Callie borrowed some money from her friend Drew to buy lunch.

_____

_____

_____

_____

_____

_____

_____

_____

_____

_____

_____

_____

_____

_____

_____

_____

_____

_____

_____

When Did It Happen?

Directions Read the paragraphs below. They tell a story using present tense verbs. Rewrite the story on the lines. Change the verbs to past tense.

Adam has a job interview at Ben's Bookstore. He introduces himself to the store manager, Ms. Lorenzo. They talk about his work experience. Adam tells about his job at the library. Ms. Lorenzo thanks Adam. She says that she will call him soon.

As he leaves, Adam feels good about the interview. The next day, he receives a call. Ms. Lorenzo asks him to start work that weekend. Adam is happy to have the job.

_____

_____

_____

_____

_____

_____

_____

_____

_____

_____

_____

_____

_____

_____

_____

_____

Creating Dialogue

Directions Rewrite the conversation below. Each time someone different begins to speak, start a new paragraph. Add the correct punctuation and capitalization.

did you see that asked Derek I sure did said Sonia and I could not believe my eyes Derek continued why would anyone wear his glasses hanging from just one ear? maybe he started to take them off said Sonia and forgot halfway. or maybe laughed Derek that is how he keeps from losing his glasses

_____

_____

_____

_____

_____

_____

_____

_____

_____

_____

_____

_____

_____

_____

_____

_____

_____

_____

Knowing When to Use Quotation Marks

Directions Change each indirect quotation to a direct quotation. Write the direct quotation on the line. Change any words that need to be changed. Add the needed punctuation and capital letters.

EXAMPLE Kristin said that she was hungry.   _Kristin said, "I am hungry."_

1. Mr. Womack asked if anyone had lost a pair of gloves.

   _____

2. Sam replied that the gloves were Megan's.

   _____

3. My sister said that I could borrow her sweater.

   _____

4. Mom asked if I had cleaned the bathroom.

   _____

5. I said that I had not, but I would do it after school.

   _____

6. Mrs. Davis reminded us that our unit test would be Friday.

   _____

7. Van asked me if I wanted to study with him Wednesday.

   _____

8. Bree said that she forgot to buy pencils and paper.

   _____

9. I said that she could borrow paper from me today.

   _____

10. Lynn said that Bree is forgetful.

   _____

Writing a Short Answer to a Test Question

Directions Write a short answer for each question. Write your answers in sentences. You may use a reference book.

1. What did Benjamin Franklin invent?

_____

_____

_____

2. Where is Yellowstone National Park?

_____

_____

_____

3. Who was Edgar Allan Poe?

_____

_____

_____

4. Where was the first permanent English colonial settlement in America?

_____

_____

_____

5. Which planet is closest to the sun?

_____

_____

_____

6. What is the capital of the United States?

_____

_____

_____

7. Who was Christopher Columbus?

_____

_____

_____

8. What is the Pulitzer Prize?

_____

_____

_____

9. Who was the first president of the United States?

_____

_____

_____

10. When did the Japanese bomb Pearl Harbor?

_____

_____

_____

Planning an Essay Answer

Directions Read the prompt carefully and answer the questions that
follow. Write your answers in sentences.

Prompt Twenty years ago, no one knew that everyone would be using
computers in their daily lives. No one knew that cell phones would be
everyday technology. Imagine the next important invention. Then write an
essay about it. Use another sheet of paper if you need more room to write.

1. What is the invention? Write one sentence identifying the invention
   and telling what it will do._____

   _____

2. How will this invention change the way people do things?
   List a few ways. _____

   _____

3. What are some good effects of this invention?

   _____

   _____

4. What are some negative effects of this invention?

   _____

   _____

5. Write a topic sentence that expresses the main idea for a paragraph
   about this invention. Your sentence should express opinion.

   _____

   _____

6. Organize your supporting ideas into several sentences that will be the
   body of your essay. _____

   _____

7. Write a one-sentence summary or conclusion for your essay.

   _____

8. Check your grammar and spelling and correct any errors.

9. Copy your essay onto another sheet of paper.

Writing a Report

Directions Use the writing clues to write a report about a book, movie, or TV show. Choose a book, movie, or show that you have read or seen.

1. Give the title of the book and the author. For a movie or TV show, just give the title.

2. Describe the setting. Tell where and when the story or show took place.

3. Describe the major characters.

4. Tell something about the plot, the events that happen in the story or show.

5. Give your opinion of the book, movie, or show. Tell why you think it is interesting, what you liked about it, or what you did not like about it.

Create a Personal Letter

Directions Write a personal letter to a friend or a relative on the lines below. This letter may be an invitation, a thank-you, or just a letter to keep in touch. Remember to include the five parts of a personal letter: date, salutation (greeting), body, closing, and signature.

Take a Message

When you take a message, be sure that it is complete. Remember, a message should include the following information:

- The time and date that you wrote the message
- The name of the person who gave you the information
- The information needed by the person who will receive the message
- Your name, to show who wrote the message

Directions Identify the information that is missing from each of the following messages. Write your answers on the lines.

EXAMPLE Dad, I'm going to the movies. I'll see you later.
              <u>time, date, when he or she will be back, and who left the</u>
              <u>message</u>

1. Derek, we were supposed to go to the movies. — Sarah

_____

_____

2. Mom, my teacher called. She'll call back later. — Derek

_____

_____

3. Mr. Smith, I have a question about the assignment. I'll stop by later.

_____

_____

4. Eliza, Amber called. She wants you to go shopping. Call her back.

_____

_____

5. Sarah, Derek called. — Dad

_____

_____

Understanding Electronic Mail (E-Mail) Messages

Directions Use the sample e-mail message to answer the questions.

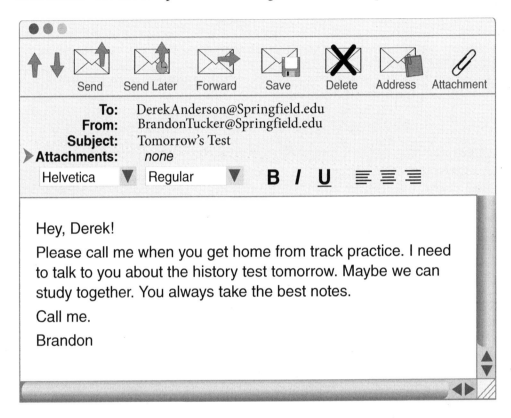

1. Who will receive this e-mail?

_____

2. Who sent it?

_____

3. What is Brandon's complete e-mail address?

_____

4. What is the name of Derek's ISP?

_____

5. What does Brandon want Derek to do?

_____

Parts of a Business Letter

Directions Decide whether these greetings and closings are appropriate
for a business letter. Write yes or no on the line following each one.

1. Dear Derek, _____

2. Cordially, _____

3. Colleagues: _____

4. Your sister, _____

5. Dear Dr. Smith: _____

6. Your friend, _____

7. Yours truly, _____

8. Dear Aunt Betsy, _____

9. Sincerely, _____

10. Love, _____

Directions Name the eight parts of a business letter. Circle the five parts
that are also included in personal letters.

11. _____

12. _____

13. _____

14. _____

15. _____

16. _____

17. _____

18. _____

Directions Name two ways in which a business letter is different from a
personal letter.

19. _____

_____

_____

_____

20. _____

_____

_____

_____

Addresses on Envelopes

Directions Some sample addresses appear below. All of them are incorrect. Rewrite each one correctly on the lines at right.

1. Tony Pierce

   Dartmouth Ct. 17

   Trenton, NJ 08601

2. Janet Lahney

   Apt. 13

   College Park, MD 20740

   92 Westland Drive

3. Crystal Enterprises

   Valerie Armstrong

   67 Tulip Drive

   19050 Lansdowne, PA

4. Managing Editor

   Fashion Trends

   Sartoga avenue 4210

   95129

   CA San Jose

5. clayton young

   Cumberland MD 21502

   517 Louisville Lane

Using Memo Form

Directions Read the following two messages. Rewrite each one in memo form.

September 10, 2007

Dear Mrs. Smith,

Please excuse John Hall today at 1:00 P.M. He has a doctor's appointment this afternoon at 1:30.

Mrs. K. Hall

May 5, 2007

Dear Mr. White,

The student body would like to see more school spirit and involvement. We would like to plan a special Springfield High Sports Day. Would you please help us in any way that you can?

Amber Choy

MEMO

Date: _____

To: _____

From: _____

Subject: _____

_____

_____

_____

_____

_____

_____

MEMO

Date: _____

To: _____

From: _____

Subject: _____

_____

_____

_____

_____

_____

_____

Expressing Opinion in a Report

Directions Find the sentence or sentences in each paragraph that express the writer's opinion. Write the sentence(s) on the lines.

1. "When in the course of human events, it becomes necessary for one people to dissolve the political bands." These are the opening words of the Declaration of Independence. It states the reasons why the American colonists believed the colonies should be independent. This is one of the most important and well-written documents in American history.

_____

_____

_____

2. Chameleons are among the best-known and most interesting lizards. These slow-moving lizards can change their color. A chameleon's color might be greenish yellow, off-white, or spotty brown. The changes happen in reaction to light or temperature.

_____

_____

_____

3. Africa is a land of natural wonders that attracts tourists. It has the Nile River, the world's longest river. It has the snow-capped Mount Kilimanjaro. Victoria Falls is an amazing sight. Yet, the biggest and most wonderful natural attraction of all is Africa's wildlife.

_____

_____

_____

4. Our school offers many different activities and clubs. All are a great way to meet friends with the same interests. Science club, debate club, and Spanish club are a few of the academic organizations. Sports activities include basketball and soccer. Theater and band are among the arts organizations.

_____

_____

_____

5. It is at the bottom of the earth. It is a cold and unwelcoming world. It is hard to believe that anyone would be willing to endure such severe conditions. Yet many scientists work in Antarctica.

_____

_____

_____

Topic Selection

Directions Read each pair of topics. Decide which one is broad and which one is narrow. Write *broad* or *narrow* on the lines.

EXAMPLE **A** Cancer   broad
                  B Treatment for cancer   narrow

1. **A** The first president, George Washington   _____
   B Presidents   _____

2. **A** Election process of Supreme Court judges   _____
   B Judges   _____

3. **A** Nutrition   _____
   B Vitamin deficiencies   _____

4. **A** Heart disease   _____
   B Disease   _____

5. **A** United States history   _____
   B The Civil War   _____

6. **A** Computers   _____
   B Selecting a computer   _____

7. **A** Historical sites in Washington, D.C.   _____
   B Washington, D.C.   _____

8. **A** Education   _____
   B Funds from the federal government for education   _____

9. **A** Zebras   _____
   B Animals of Africa   _____

10. **A** Whole grains   _____
    B Brown rice   _____

Using Reference Materials

Directions Write the reference book you would use to find the answer to each question. Choose from *almanac, atlas, encyclopedia,* or *biographical dictionary.*

1. Which states border the Mississippi River?

_____

2. Who is Nelson Mandela?

_____

3. Who won the World Series in 2000?

_____

4. What highways cross Texas?

_____

5. Discuss the history of computers.

_____

Directions Use the information in the catalog entry to answer the questions.

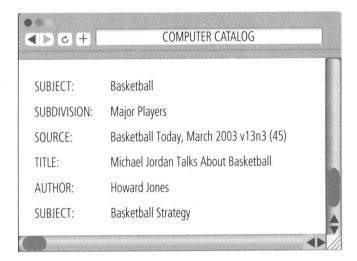

COMPUTER CATALOG

SUBJECT:	Basketball
SUBDIVISION:	Major Players
SOURCE:	Basketball Today, March 2003 v13n3 (45)
TITLE:	Michael Jordan Talks About Basketball
AUTHOR:	Howard Jones
SUBJECT:	Basketball Strategy

6. Who is the author of this article?

_____

7. What is this article probably about?

_____

8. What is the title of the magazine?

_____

9. In which volume does this article appear?

_____

10. How long is this article?

_____

Searching the Internet

Directions Read each question. Write the keyword or keywords that would help you find the answer.

1. How do you play the game of chess?

_____

2. How long did the American Civil War last?

_____

3. Are tomatoes fruits?

_____

4. What are the titles of Gwendolyn Brooks's poems?

_____

5. What is the former name of Mumbai?

_____

6. Where is the world's tallest building?

_____

7. What organization did César Chávez help form?

_____

8. Who played left field for the New York Yankees in 2007?

_____

9. When did the production *Cats* first play on Broadway?

_____

10. With what ballet companies did Mikhail Baryshnikov dance?

_____

Directions Find the word in the Word Bank to complete each sentence.

11. For searching the Internet using words or phrases, you use a computer program called a _____.

12. Web sites operated by government agencies and _____ are usually good sources.

13. An example of a _____ is www.hplibrary.org.

14. A _____ is a computer program that allows you to use the information on Internet Web sites.

15. A _____ is a word or phrase you use to search for Internet information.

Word Bank
browser
educational institutions
keyword
search engine
Web address

Notes

Directions Read the paragraph. Take five notes on the paragraph. Write your notes on the lines.

Wolfgang Amadeus Mozart is one of the world's most important composers. He lived during the eighteenth century in Austria. He was born in 1756 and died in 1791. Mozart composed some of the most famous operas, including *The Magic Flute*, *The Marriage of Figaro*, and *Don Giovanni*. Mozart was a child prodigy. At a very young age, he performed on the piano all over Europe. A movie about his life titled *Amadeus* won the Academy Award for best picture in 1984.

1. _____

2. _____

3. _____

4. _____

5. _____

Directions Paraphrase your notes in a paragraph of your own about Mozart. Write your paraphrased notes on the lines.

_____

_____

_____

_____

_____

Correcting an Outline

Directions Use Outline A as a guide. Rewrite Outline B in the correct form on another sheet of paper. Use correct punctuation. Indent the lines correctly. Capitalize the first word of each topic and any proper nouns.

EXAMPLE

Outline A	**Outline B**
Nicaragua	**United Nations**

I. Introduction	I. Introduction
A. Location	a. location
B. Size	B. Buildings
1. Population	II. General Assembly
2. Area	A. composed of
II. Geographical features	b. sessions
A. Atlantic and Pacific coasts	C. Budget and apportion expenses
B. The Cordillera Mountains	3 Security Council
C. Volcanoes	A. Number of members
III. Agriculture and industry	b. purpose
A. Chief crops	4. Economic and Social Council
1. Bananas	A. Number of members
2. Cotton	b. purpose
B. Minerals	V. Trusteeship Council
1. Gold	VI Secretariat
2. Silver	VII International Court of Justice
3. Copper	a Function
IV. Currency	B Election
V. Languages	1. Term
VI. Summary and conclusions	2. Method
	8 Summary and conclusion

Organizing Topics to Write a Report

Directions Follow the steps to organize the topics in a logical order. Use outline form with correct punctuation.

Step 1 Identify the main topics.

Step 2 Identify the subtopics that belong with each main topic.

Step 3 Write the topics and subtopics in correct outline form on the lines.

A Typical Home Office

Bookshelves _____

Tape _____

Chair _____

Computer _____

Desk _____

Modem _____

Office furniture _____

Paper _____

Pens and pencils _____

Printer _____

Stapler _____

Supplies _____

Telephone _____

Types of equipment _____

Work table _____

Adding Transitions

Directions Part of revising a report involves adding transitions. Transitions help connect the ideas of sentences and paragraphs. Read the sentences below. Each sentence is missing a transition. Add a few words or a sentence to connect the two thoughts.

1. Sputnik, a Soviet satellite, reached space in 1957.
In 1969, man walked on the moon.

_____

_____

2. Scientists realized these rockets were the best way of getting man to space.
Riding on top of a rocket was dangerous.

_____

_____

3. The third part of the trip was re-entering earth's atmosphere.
Splashdown was when the capsule landed in the ocean.

_____

_____

4. The space shuttle has given NASA some of its most spectacular achievements.
Two space shuttles, the Challenger and the Columbia, have exploded and killed their crews.

_____

_____

5. Some people think NASA should send people to Mars.
There are many challenges left for NASA to solve.

_____

_____